A Painful History of Medicine

Pox, Pus † Plague
a history of disease and infection

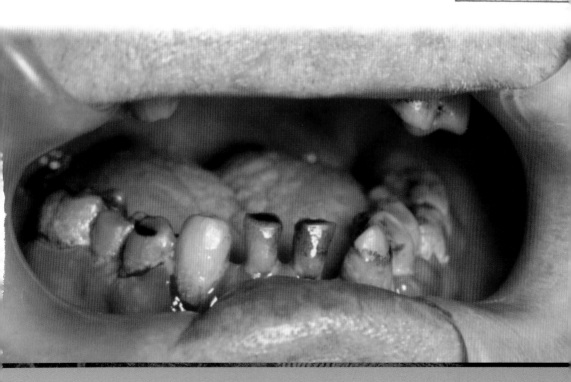

John Townsend

www.raintreepublishers.co.uk

Visit our website to find out more information about **Raintree** books.

To order:
- ☎ Phone 44 (0) 1865 888113
- 🖹 Send a fax to 44 (0) 1865 314091
- 💻 Visit the Raintree bookshop at **www.raintreepublishers.co.uk** to browse our catalogue and order online.

First published in Great Britain by Raintree, Halley Court, Jordan Hill, Oxford OX2 8EJ, part of Harcourt Education.
Raintree is a registered trademark of Harcourt Education Ltd.

Editorial: Melanie Copland and Kate Buckingham
Design: Michelle Lisseter and Bridge Creative Services Ltd
Picture Research: Hannah Taylor and Ginny Stroud-Lewis
Production: Duncan Gilbert

Originated by Dot Gradations
Printed and bound in China
by South China Printing Company

ISBN 1 844 43751 5
09 08 07 06 05
10 9 8 7 6 5 4 3 2 1

British Library Cataloguing in Publication Data
Townsend, John
Disease – (A Painful History of Medicine)
616'.009
A full catalogue record for this book is available from the British Library.

Acknowledgements
Alamy Images pp. **16** (Medical on Line), **50–51** (image100); Art Directors and Trip pp. **7**, **13**, **21** (Helene Rogers); Bridgeman Art Library pp. **14** (Alinari Osterreichische Nationalbibliothek, Vienna, Austria), **16–17** (Guildhall Library, Corporation of London, UK), **19**, **22** (Private Collection), **36** (Archives Charmet); (Chicago Department of Water Management) pp. **24–25**; Corbis pp. **6** (Lester V Bergman), **8** (Historical Picture Archive), **11** (Mark Peterson), **12** (Bettmann), **23** (Hulton-Deutsch Collection), **24**, **26–27**, **30–31** (Bettmann), **32** (CDC/PHIL), **35** (Hulton-Deutsch Collection), **39** (Bettman), **42–43** (Phil Schermeister), **43** (Gideon Mandel), **47** (Children's Hospital & Medical Center), **48–49** (Reuters), **49** (Alan Hindle), **53**; Frank Graham p. **9**; GettyImages/ PhotoDisc pp. **50**, **51**; Hulton Archive pp. **38–39**; Kobal Collection pp. **36–37**; Mary Evans Picture Library p. **28**; Medical on Line pp. **10**, **19**, **20**, **29**, **33**, **34–35**, **40–41**; Science Photo Library pp. **4–5** (Custom Medical Stock Photo), **10–11** (Mauro Fermariello), **14–15** (St Mary's Hospital Medical School), **18** (John Walsh), **22–23** (Dr Klaus Boller), **34** (Custom Medical Stock Photo), **41** (St Mary's Hospital Medical School), **44** (R Umesh Chandran), **44–45** (Andrew Syred), **45** (Volker Steger), **46** (Colin Cuthbert); Wellcome Library, London pp. **27**, **28**, **30**, **32–33**.

Cover photograph of woman in iron lung reproduced with permission of Corbis/Bettmann

Contents

Any words appearing in the text in bold,
like this, are explained in the glossary.
You can also look out for them in the Word
bank at the bottom of each page.

Under attack

On the defence

Our bodies have to fight disease all the time. Our **immune system** attacks all the tiny **organisms** that want to invade us. If our immune system fails, we become ill. Unless our bodies can fight back again the disease will win.

Our bodies do strange things. When they work well, we do not think about them much. When they go wrong, we soon know. It is amazing that our bodies do not go wrong more often. After all, they are always under attack. Your body is fighting disease all the time.

From the common cold to nasty infections that give us oozing **boils** or rotting flesh, diseases are bad news. Today we know how to fight some of them. We have had to learn through centuries of pain, **pus, pox, plagues** and pimples!

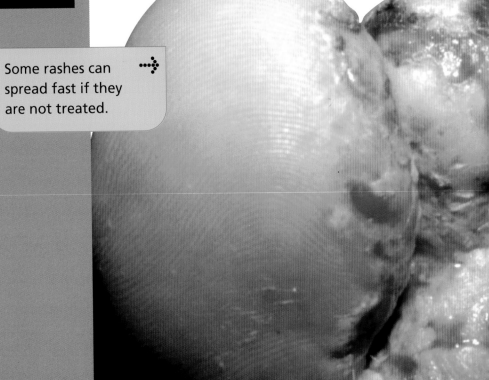

Some rashes can spread fast if they are not treated.

Word bank

bacteria   group of tiny living things, some can cause disease
organism   living cell or group of cells

Why?

Doctors throughout history have wondered about disease and why some spread so fast.

Two big questions doctors once asked were:
1. *How do people catch diseases?*
2. *How can they be cured?*

Fast facts

We now know many diseases are spread by:
- **Bacteria** – tiny living things that enter the body in dirty food, water or air.
- **Viruses** – tiny living things that break into the body's cells.

Find out later...

Which disease causes black vomit?

What is leprosy?

What diseases do people fear today?

virus tiny living thing that breaks into the body's cells and can cause disease

Ancient times

Many diseases are caught from other people. Ten thousand years ago, humans first began to live together in large groups or **tribes**. Diseases could then spread easily from one person to another.

Spreading disease

Sometimes people caught diseases from their animals. Animal food and **dung** attracted insects and rats, which spread more disease. Then when tribes moved to new areas, they passed their diseases on to other tribes.

Coughs and sneezes spread diseases!

Word bank   bowel   part of the intestine where waste is held before being let out of the body

Egyptians

The ancient Egyptians believed some diseases were caused by blockages in the body. To unblock themselves they tried to vomit or open the **bowels** by eating **senna**. They also cut themselves to bleed away the disease. Egyptian writings from 3500 years ago told how to treat an ill person:

> If he is ill in his arm then make him vomit by feeding him fish and beer. Cover his fingers with watermelon until he is healed. If he is ill in the bowel, the blockage must be cleared.

Viruses

The Egyptians were right to think that blood could carry disease. One thousand viruses can live in one **red blood cell**. And there are 5 million red blood cells in one drop of blood!

Marks on the face of a 3000-year-old Egyptian mummy are likely to have been left by the **smallpox** disease.

tribe group of people living closely together, sharing the same beliefs and customs

Nearly 2500 years ago the Greek doctor Hippocrates said the body was made up of 4 fluids, or humours. These were blood, **phlegm**, yellow **bile** and black bile. Greeks thought disease was caused by too much or too little of one of these fluids.

Doctors let blood out of veins for centuries as they thought it was good for the patient.

Greeks

Over 2000 years ago the Greeks and the Romans had their share of **plagues**. These deadly diseases spread quickly across large areas. Around 2400 years ago a plague killed a third of the people living in Athens in Greece.

The Greeks saw how the weather, soil and water made a difference to people's health. Fewer people suffered disease on high ground. Marshy lowlands were seen to be less healthy by Greeks. They were right – this was where **mosquitoes** bred. These insects spread deadly **malaria**.

Word bank

bile   fluid made by the liver to help digestion
hygiene   standards of cleanliness

Romans

The Romans knew that dirty water was unhealthy. They knew disease came with bad air, bad water, swamps and **sewage**. In fact, they built public toilets so they could flush away all their sewage. Romans used to meet friends, sit and chat, whilst all using the toilets together!

Even though they had good **hygiene**, Romans often got **worms**. These were caught from poorly cooked or dirty food. They lived inside people's bodies.

Many Romans died from plagues. One plague lasted fifteen years. It killed up to 5000 people a day in Rome alone.

Roman toilets got rid of waste safely and were good meeting places!

Bad smell

" If soldiers are allowed to stay in one place too long they are made miserable by the smell of their own excrement. The air becomes unhealthy and they catch diseases. **"**

Vegetius, a Roman writer from the 4th century.

malaria   disease that causes fevers and chills, spread by mosquito bites
phlegm   thick fluid in the lungs and throat

The Middle Ages

The **Middle Ages** was a time of disease and **superstition**. There were all kinds of strange ideas about what caused disease and how it could be cured.

Beliefs

Many people believed that disease was a punishment. If you lived a bad life you deserved to be ill. So people often had no sympathy for the sick. Many doctors believed in magic and lucky charms to cure illness. A few herbs or spells might be the best help you could expect.

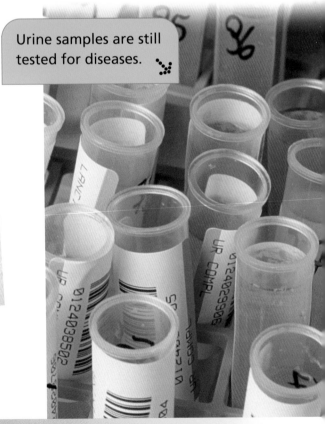

Urine samples are still tested for diseases.

Scrofula was a disease that often affected victims' necks in the Middle Ages.

Word bank

Middle Ages   period of history roughly between AD 500 and AD 1500

Finding a cure

Many **monks** grew and sold herbs as drugs. Local witches also used all kinds of plants to treat disease. They were probably just as good as doctors at curing illness!

One cure for **boils** used by doctors was to rub on herbs mixed with pig **dung**.

*"This will cure boils and the **pus** will disappear."*
From a 13th-century medical book.

Many doctors looked at the colour of a patient's **urine** to see what it showed about the patient. Today, doctors still look at urine samples – but the science is a little more precise now!

Tough times

During the Middle Ages, many diseases killed children. Flu, **plague, smallpox, tuberculosis** and **whooping cough** killed nearly half of all children under the age of fifteen.

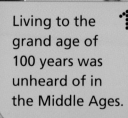

Living to the grand age of 100 years was unheard of in the Middle Ages.

superstition belief based on magic or chance
urine liquid passed from the body, usually pale yellow

Around 1330, a deadly plague began in China. Once people fell ill, they infected others very quickly by sneezing. By 1350 travellers visiting China had taken the plague to most of Europe, where it killed 65 million people.

The Black Death

The 1300s were a terrible time for disease all over the world. People lived in fear that they would be the next to be struck by the dreaded **plague**. The disease became known as the Black Death because people's skin often turned dark purple.

People had no idea that **bacteria** in fleas spread the disease. Fleas drank the blood of diseased rats, and then hopped on to people, cats and dogs. When the fleas bit, the disease passed into the wound. Deadly bacteria soon got into the victim's bloodstream.

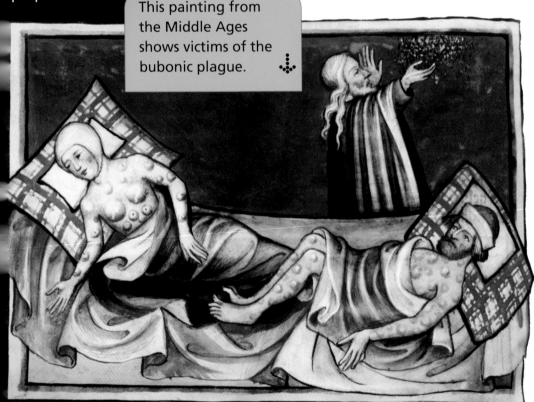

This painting from the Middle Ages shows victims of the bubonic plague.

Word bank

buboes   swollen areas in the groin and armpits
fever   very high body temperature caused by illness

Lumps and blood

Victims of the Black Death got headaches, aching joints, **fever** and vomiting. It took between one and seven days for **glands** to become swollen and painful. The glands were called **buboes**, which led to the name bubonic plague.

Italian writer Boccaccio wrote:

> It began with swellings in the groin and armpit. Some of these were as big as apples and some were shaped like eggs.

Some other types of plague were spread by sneezes or even on people's clothes. These victims dribbled slimy **saliva** full of blood from their mouths and noses.

Pesky pigs

Two pigs pressed their snouts into the rags of a man who had just died from the plague. The pigs picked up the rags with their teeth and shook them. Within a short time, they both began to shake and fell dead on the ground.

Italian writer Boccaccio, (1313 to 1375).

Fleas on rats carried the dreaded plague. •:•:

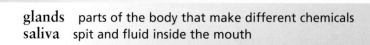

glands   parts of the body that make different chemicals
saliva   spit and fluid inside the mouth

Old and new worlds

The **Middle Ages** was a time of exploration. Sailors set out to find new lands. They brought back new treasures but also new **bacteria** and disease. The sailors spread these diseases to people on different islands. The islanders died quickly, even from common colds, as they had no **immunity**.

In 1492, the explorer Christopher Columbus was the first European to sail his ship to an island in the Bahamas. He called it San Salvador. The **Native Americans** there began to die in their hundreds. Measles, **smallpox** and flu spread quickly among them.

Sick sailors

Sailors began to travel the world in the Middle Ages. But a sailor's life was not very healthy. It was not just sea-sickness that caused their misery. Sailors often fell ill for other reasons. Insect bites, bad food and bacteria made life on a ship deadly.

Scurvy makes gums painful and swollen.

Life on board ship was far from healthy in the Middle Ages.

Word bank   **immunity**   the body's protection against disease

Poor food

Not all diseases were spread by bacteria. Food could also lead to terrible illness. Sailors out at sea for months on end often ate a poor diet of ship's biscuits, usually full of maggots.

A poor diet could cause a disease called **scurvy**. The skin went black with **ulcers**, teeth fell out and the gums rotted. Victims often went mad and died. But their misery could easily have been cured – by eating fruit. Scurvy was caused by a lack of **vitamin** C.

British sailors then took lime juice on their ships to keep scurvy at bay. They got the nickname "Limeys" because of this.

Scurvy

Vasco da Gama was a famous sailor from Portugal. Sixty-five per cent of his crew died of scurvy while sailing to India in 1499.

Magellan was another sailor from Portugal. About 50 per cent of his sailors died while crossing the Pacific Ocean.

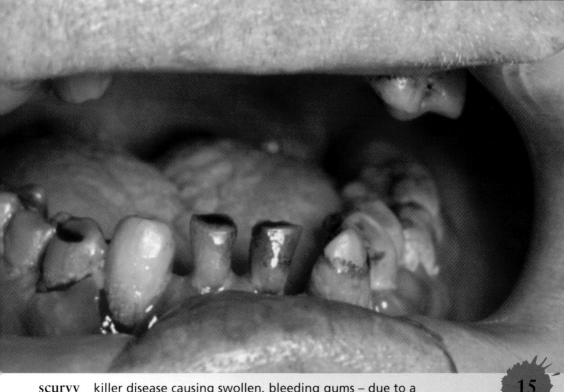

scurvy   killer disease causing swollen, bleeding gums – due to a lack of vitamin C

Epidemic

A doctor's protection against the plague would have been useless against fleas!

Each century has had a major **epidemic**. Nothing can stop some diseases taking hold and spreading out of control.

The 1600s

The 1660s were not a good time for London. In 1665 bubonic **plague** killed up to 7000 people a week. Within a few months, 55,000 people had died. That was about 20 per cent of the total population of London.

Many people left the city for the countryside, where they hoped they would be safer. But they took the disease with them and it spread even more.

The great plague

Doctors were at great risk during the plague. They wore leather gowns that were meant to protect them. The long beak-like nose was filled with herbs and the eye-holes were covered with glass in the hope of keeping out smells. But it was not smells that spread the plague!

Word bank   epidemic   outbreak of a disease that spreads quickly over a wide area

On the move

In 1665 a delivery of cloth was sent a long way from London to the village of Eyam. The man who received it died four days later. Infected fleas arrived on the cloth and brought the plague with them. After a few weeks, only about half of the 350 villagers were still alive.

In 1666 the plague was still spreading through London. Then a huge fire swept through the city. It burnt down 13,000 houses in 4 days. The flames also killed thousands of rats and their fleas. The fire stopped the plague at last.

Graveyard

Skeletons of plague victims have been found in London. **Mass graves** from 1665 show that bodies had been buried in a hurry, all piled in at once.

The great fire of London destroyed much of the city, including diseases.

mass graves   huge graves where lots of people were buried together

Mosquitoes drink blood. When they stab the skin to feed, they can pass viruses into the victim's blood. That is how yellow fever spreads.

Yellow fever causes bleeding in the stomach. Juices in the stomach then turn black because of the blood.

Yellow fever

Yellow fever was another disease that spread on ships across the world. **Mosquitoes** bit sailors and gave them the deadly **virus**. When ships sailed on to new lands, other mosquitoes bit the infected sailors. These mosquitoes then carried the virus to more humans, and so the disease spread.

In 1793 a yellow fever **epidemic** hit Philadelphia, USA. It killed roughly 4000 people. For the next 30 years yellow fever was one of the most feared diseases in US ports.

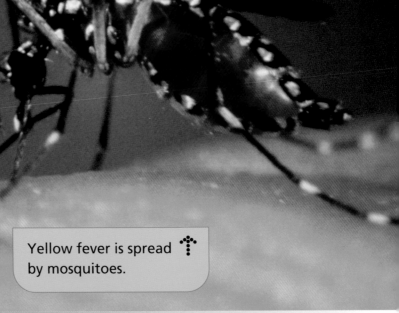

Yellow fever is spread by mosquitoes.

Word bank vaccine medicine to make the body defend itself against a disease

Black vomit

Yellow fever was also called yellow death because it caused liver damage. This turned the skin bright yellow.

It had other nasty effects, too. When a girl died of the disease in Memphis, Tennessee in 1897, her uncle said that her screams could be heard right down the street.

"Her tongue and lips were dark and cracked, and blood oozed from the mouth and nose. The most terrible thing was the black vomit. It was as black as ink."

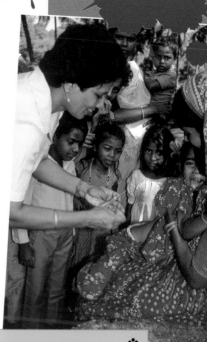

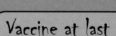 Being protected against yellow fever in India.

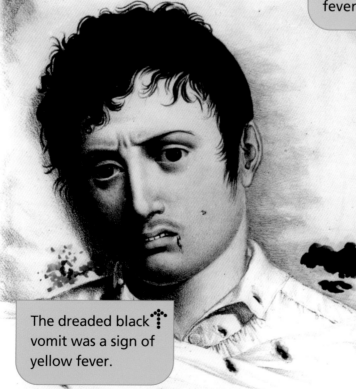

The dreaded black vomit was a sign of yellow fever.

Vaccine at last

Scientists in New York developed a **vaccine** for yellow fever in the 1930s. Because of this vaccine, yellow fever is no longer the epidemic killer it once was. A single dose of the vaccine protects someone for at least ten years.

yellow fever   disease spread by mosquitoes, causing fever, aching limbs and yellow skin

Measles

Measles is a **virus** that can be spread by sneezing. You can also catch measles by sharing cups or spoons. It causes a rash, cough and **fever**. It can also kill a person.

The 1800s

- In 1846, a measles **epidemic** affected nearly 80 per cent of people living on the Faeroe Islands, near Iceland.
- During the American Civil War (from 1861 to 1865), there were nearly 100,000 cases of measles among 4 million soldiers. Almost 3000 died.
- In 1875, British sailors took measles to Fiji by mistake. Nearly 40,000 islanders died.

Measles is still common in poorer countries. There are about 40 million cases each year, with more than a million deaths. **Vaccines** for measles were first used in the 1960s, but poor countries cannot afford these expensive drugs.

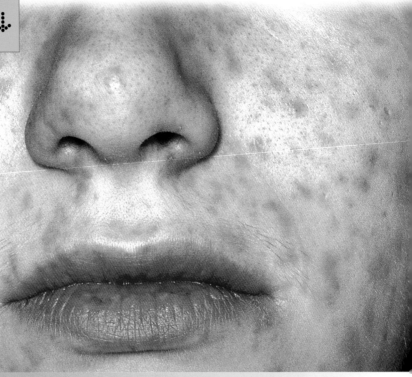

A measles rash can be very itchy.

Word bank   antibiotic   substance made from bacteria that kills other harmful bacteria

Leprosy

Leprosy is often thought to affect poor people living in dirty places. In fact, it can affect anyone. Sores and **tumours** can destroy the face, often resulting in blindness. Leprosy also causes areas all over the body to go numb. It can spread through coughing and sneezing.

In 1995, there were about 1.8 million cases of leprosy in the world. Most of these were in South-East Asia, Africa and South America.

Progress

- Leprosy **bacteria** were first discovered in 1873.
- In 1940, an **antibiotic** was discovered that worked against the leprosy bacteria.
- In the 1980s a drug called MDT was first used to cure leprosy.

Some people in South America, Africa and South-East Asia still suffer from leprosy.

Today leprosy can be cured – as long as people can afford the right drugs.

0   3000   6000 Miles

0   6000 Kilometres

Arctic Ocean

Asia

North America

Europe

Atlantic Ocean

Pacific Ocean

Pacific Ocean

Africa

South America

N

Indian Ocean

Oceania

Antarctica

tumour   abnormal growth or swelling in the body

Flu

Flu **epidemics** do not just kill the old and weak. They can kill healthy people too.

The 1900s

Less than a hundred years ago, a major flu **pandemic** struck. It killed millions of people across the world.

In 1918, at the end of World War 1, many people were on the move. A deadly type of flu was on the move as well. This flu killed young, healthy people. Half its victims were aged between 20 and 40.

By the end of 1918, 20 million people had died of flu. In the USA, 550,000 people died in 10 months.

Many children died from flu in the 1800s.

Word bank   **electron microscope**   microscope using electron beams to make images much larger

Fighting back

In 1918 microscopes were still unable to show the tiny flu **virus**. It was not until the 1930s that scientists developed new **electron microscopes**. At last they could see and photograph flu viruses. This was a big step towards finding out about different types of the disease. Better **vaccines** were made to fight them. But viruses can change.

Even today scientists have to be alert for new types of flu. They must be quick to send out new vaccines to stop another flu epidemic.

American police in Seattle, USA, wore masks to guard them from flu.

The flu virus can be seen under a microscope.

USA

In October 1918, 195,000 Americans died from flu.

- 851 New Yorkers died in a single day.
- In Philadelphia, the city's death rate for one single week was 700 times higher than normal.

pandemic   disease that spreads quickly across the world

Secrets in the water

We need to drink water every day. But for many people, the water they need to live may also bring death. People always thought that if the water they drank looked clean, they were safe. They were wrong.

Causing a stink

In London in the 1850s, about 250 tons of human **excrement** flowed into the River Thames each day. The river was also used for drinking water!

In 1858, the summer was very hot and water levels dropped. The river became known as the "Great Stink". London was a breeding ground for disease.

Dung

Horses were once used everywhere. By 1900, 10 million tons of horse **dung** had to be cleared from English towns each year. This was a breeding ground for flies and rats.

Human manure was put into cesspits. But these seeped into the surrounding soil and into **wells** so drinking water became **polluted**.

Maxwell Street was once a **slum** area in Chicago.

Word bank

cesspit   hole dug to hold waste and sewage
pollute   make air or water dirty or unsafe

Chicago

In the 1800s, no one realized the link between **sewage** and disease. People in Chicago, USA, used the river for water and as a waste tip. Animals were kept in alleys and their manure was dumped into Chicago's streets. Rainwater washed this into the river and **cesspits**. This mixture would seep into the water supply.

Diseases like **typhoid** and **cholera** spread quickly. It was not until big sewer pipes were built to carry waste away that Chicago finally became clean and safe.

Animal waste

More than 2 million cows, sheep and pigs were brought to London markets in 1876. In some parts of London there were far more pigs than people. That was a lot of manure to clog the streets and drain into the water supply!

Chicago needed huge sewers to make the city clean and safe.

well   hole dug down into the ground for getting water

Typhoid

Typhoid fever is deadly. It begins like flu and in a week, a red rash appears on the chest and back. Then comes **diarrhoea** and a dry mouth. The disease can kill in a few weeks.

During the 1800s many doctors thought typhoid was carried in the bad smells of dirty cities. They did not know the dirty water was actually the problem.

Chicago had more typhoid deaths in the 1880s than any other city in the world. It was at this time that the scientist Carl Eberth discovered the **bacteria** that caused the disease. The cure came many years later.

Easily spread

Typhoid is spread in dirty drinking water or on unwashed hands. People can pass it on to others without becoming infected themselves. Flies can carry typhoid from **sewage** on to food.

Mary Mallon was locked up in an institution until she died in 1938.

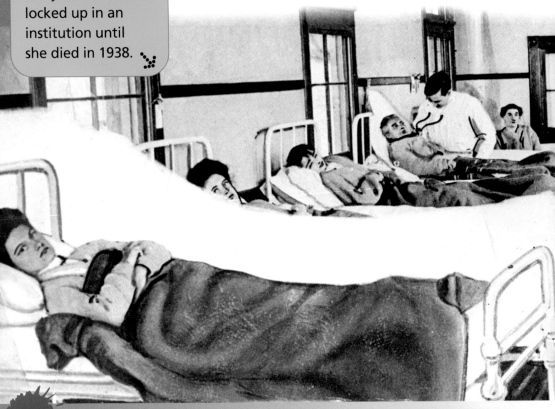

Word bank   diarrhoea   the need to use the toilet very often (when waste is too liquid)

Dangerous lady

In 1906, there were 3467 cases of typhoid in New York, with 639 deaths. The most famous typhoid carrier was Mary Mallon.

"Typhoid Mary" was hired as a cook in a New York house in the early 1900s. Within weeks, six people in the house caught typhoid. Doctors gave Mary tests. They found she was carrying the disease but she was not affected herself. She was told to keep away from kitchens.

Twenty people caught typhoid at a New York hospital in 1915. The police found that the cook was Mary Mallon and they took her away to be locked up.

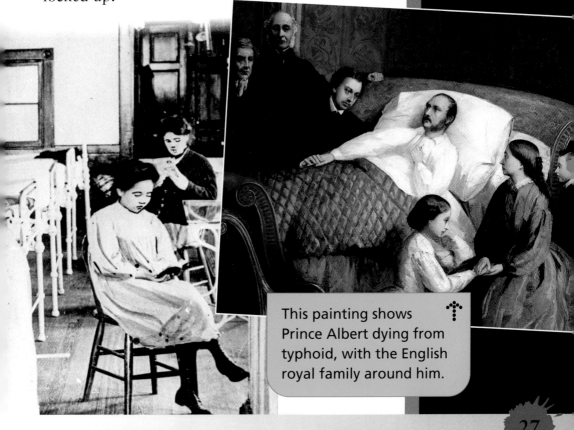

This painting shows Prince Albert dying from typhoid, with the English royal family around him.

Doctor John Snow, who discovered that cholera was carried in dirty water.

Cholera

Cholera is a disease that attacks the **intestines**. Victims have severe **diarrhoea** and vomiting. Today cholera can be cured if treated quickly. This means getting fluid and salts back into the body quickly. Then a course of **antibiotics** can kill the **bacteria**.

In the past, doctors could do little about cholera. In 1854, it killed 6 per cent of the people of Chicago. About 60 people died of the disease each day. The city's streets were lined with coffins.

Recent cholera epidemics

- **1971:** Bangladesh, Asia – 6500 deaths
- **1991:** Peru, South America – 3000 deaths
- **1994:** Rwanda, Africa – 20,000 deaths

The disease spreads when drinking water becomes **polluted** by sewers. Many poor countries do not have clean water supplies – cholera still exists in these countries.

A cartoon from 1858 showed Father Thames bringing his children **Diphtheria**, Cholera and **Scrofula** to London.

Word bank

intestine   part of the body that goes from the stomach to the bowel, where food is digested

Discovery

In 1832 cholera spread through Europe and America. In Paris, 7000 people died in a few months.

A British doctor, John Snow, was sure cholera was caught from water. But he could not convince other doctors about this. Everyone thought cholera spread in smelly air.

Ideas changed after a mother washed her baby's nappy in a London **well** in 1854. A cholera **epidemic** began.

John Snow proved that the 616 victims who died all drank from the same well. His work led to the discovery of cholera bacteria 30 years later.

Fast facts

In the 20th century, cholera killed over 20 million people in India alone.

Cholera bacteria are now known to live in dirty water.

Polio

Polio is a **virus** that damages the **nervous system.** It has killed and disabled people throughout history.

Children often caught polio at swimming pools or from infected drinking water. Many victims died from being unable to breathe. Other victims lost the use of their legs. They could only walk with crutches. **Epidemics** all around the world were common until **vaccines** were discovered.

Fast facts

In 1928 a machine called an iron lung was invented. Polio sufferers had to lie inside it while a pump helped them to breathe.

Children with polio needed special supports to straighten their legs.

War

Franklin Roosevelt was President of the USA in the 1930s. He caught polio when he was a child. Roosevelt called for a "War on Polio" and did a lot to help research into the disease.

In the 1940s scientists Jonas Salk and Albert Sabin worked on monkeys to develop a vaccine for polio. In 1955 they were successful. Their work has saved the lives of millions of children. The USA became polio-free in 1979.

Happy ending

Great efforts have been made to stamp out polio once and for all. In 2001, 575 million children were vaccinated in 94 countries. That year fewer than 500 polio cases were reported worldwide.

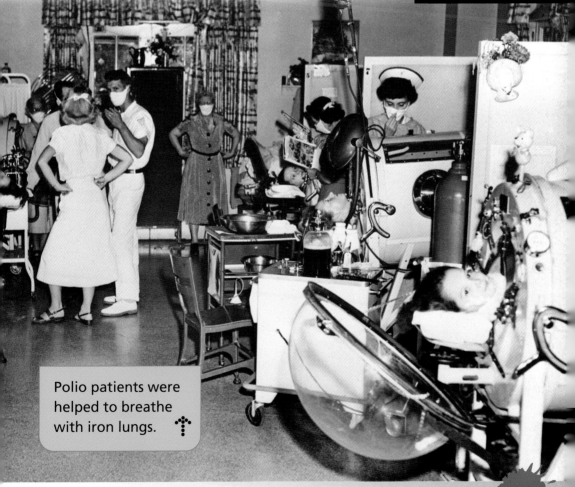

Polio patients were helped to breathe with iron lungs.

paralysis   unable to move
suffocation   unable to breathe

Great discoveries

Some people have made a huge difference in the fight against disease. Key events have led to important discoveries.

Smallpox

Smallpox was a terrible disease. It caused the skin to bubble up in nasty blisters. Victims usually died from **fever**. Smallpox was spread through direct contact with an infected person, or with their clothes or bedding. In the 18th century, smallpox killed a third of those who caught it.

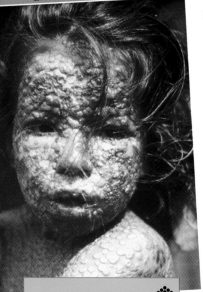

Smallpox can leave pockmarks all over the body.

Europeans who moved to the USA took smallpox with them. The disease spread and killed many **Native Americans**.

Easily spread

Smallpox was feared in the 18th century. People had the disease for about twelve days before they felt ill. They infected others without knowing. Those who survived were often left blind and scarred by deep **pockmarks**.

Fast facts

Vaccinate comes from the Latin word *vacca* meaning cow.

A cartoon from 1802 made fun of vaccination by showing that it turned patients into cows!

Word bank   **pockmark**   round scar left on the skin after a pox disease

Edward Jenner

Edward Jenner was an English doctor born in the 1700s. He noticed that milkmaids never caught smallpox. Instead they got a weak form of smallpox called cowpox.

The milkmaids got blisters on their hands from milking cows that carried the disease. Jenner thought the **pus** in these blisters protected them from catching smallpox.

He injected pus from cowpox blisters into a **volunteer** called James. Then Jenner injected him with smallpox. James became ill but in a few days he made an amazing recovery. Jenner had found out how to vaccinate people against the dreaded smallpox.

Doctor Edward Jenner.

Wiped out

- Smallpox killed between 300 and 500 million people in the 20th century.
- In the 1970s world-wide vaccination was carried out.
- In 1980 smallpox was wiped out at last.

volunteer   someone who offers to take part in something

Louis Pasteur

French scientist Louis Pasteur (below) first developed the idea that tiny living things could get into our bodies and attack us. He found that these "**bacteria**" could live in soil, water, air, plants and animals. Pasteur believed that some bacteria caused disease. He set about proving his ideas to other scientists.

Big ideas

Louis Pasteur knew all about the work done by Edward Jenner on **smallpox**. He thought that if a vaccine could be found for smallpox, then a vaccine could be found for all diseases.

Fast facts

We have Louis Pasteur to thank for our cartons of bacteria-free milk today. Pasteurised milk is heated to make it safe to drink.

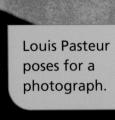

Louis Pasteur poses for a photograph.

Anthrax

Anthrax is a deadly animal disease which can pass to humans in wool, cloth and leather. Pasteur began working with anthrax bacteria. He was sure bacteria could cause disease and wanted to find ways of killing bacteria in the body.

Pasteur discovered that one kind of bacteria could attack and kill another kind. He tried this with anthrax and developed a **vaccine** for the disease.

Sheep being vaccinated against anthrax in New Guinea in 1925.

Rabies

Rabies is a deadly **virus**. People catch it by being bitten by an infected animal. The disease starts with **fever**, headache and pain around the bitten area. It leads to **spasms**, a fear of water, madness, **coma** and death.

Louis Pasteur and his team knew that rabies attacked the **nervous system** and the brain. By taking **cells** from **spinal cords** of dead victims, he made a **vaccine**. It seemed to work on animals. But would it do the same for humans?

Pasteur and his team take saliva from a dog with rabies.

This dog has rabies.

Danger

Dogs with rabies are very dangerous. Louis Pasteur needed help with his experiments to find a rabies vaccine. Members of his team had to hold down a dog while he tried to collect the **saliva**. Pasteur then studied the virus in the saliva.

Word bank   spasm   sudden, uncontrolled movement of muscles

Risk

In 1885 a dog with rabies bit a boy called Joseph. He would have died in agony if nothing was done so he was taken to Louis Pasteur who decided to try out his vaccine. It was a risk but Joseph survived and was soon well again. Pasteur now knew that his rabies vaccine worked.

The following year, about 2500 people were treated for rabies. When Pasteur died in 1895, 20,000 people had been successfully treated.

Did you know?

- Rabies is found all over the world except for Australia, Antarctica and some small islands.
- In the USA, about one person every year dies from rabies.
- Worldwide, between 45,000 and 60,000 people die each year from rabies. They do not get the vaccine in time.

spinal cord bundle of nerves that run down the backbone

Deadly lung disease

Tuberculosis (or TB) was a disease everyone feared well into the 20th century. It was a serious disease of the lungs. Coughing and sneezing meant it spread quickly in crowded **slums**.

Doctors thought TB patients needed fresh air. They often moved their beds outside – even in the snow! This did little to make patients feel better. They already had a bad cough, tiredness, no appetite and a **fever**. They often coughed up blood, too. TB was a miserable killer disease.

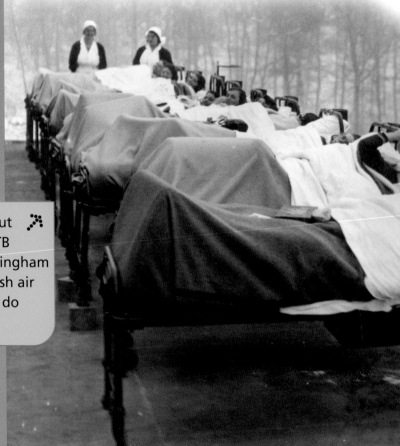

Patients were put outside at this TB hospital in Nottingham in 1933. The fresh air was thought to do them good.

Word bank   **consumption**   another name for the disease tuberculosis

Robert Koch

In 1882, the German doctor Robert Koch found the **bacteria** that caused TB. He and his team had searched for a long time and it was a great breakthrough. The following year he found the bacteria that caused **cholera**. Only then could scientists get to work on making **vaccines** for the diseases.

Robert Koch's work helped fight diseases that still killed millions of people into the 20th century. In 1891 he set up a centre for **infectious** diseases in Berlin, Germany. In 1905 Robert Koch received the famous **Nobel Prize** for his life-saving work.

TB today

Even today in the 21st century, TB kills over a million people each year. Those who live in poor, damp and crowded places can still become infected.

Doctor Robert Koch working in his science lab.

Penicillin

A great discovery in the last hundred years was a type of drug called an **antibiotic**. It changed the fight against disease forever. The drug was made from **mould**. Some mould can kill harmful **bacteria**.

The world's first antibiotic was called penicillin. Doctors began using it in the 1940s. Since then it has saved millions of lives by fighting infection. The number of children dying from **pneumonia** has fallen by 93 per cent due to penicillin.

Alexander Fleming ••••⋮• at work in his laboratory in France in 1916.

Word bank   antiseptic   substance that stops harmful bacteria growing and spreading disease

Alexander Fleming

In 1928 Alexander Fleming made history. He came back from holiday to his lab in London and found that mould had grown on a dish of pneumonia bacteria. Fleming was amazed to find the mould had killed the bacteria. This mould was called penicillin.

Soon other scientists got to work on Fleming's discovery. Howard Florey was an Australian scientist working in the UK. In 1940, he and his team found that penicillin was good at fighting all kinds of disease. Florey's team grew the mould in milk churns, lemonade bottles and bedpans. Then they tried it on a patient. It worked!

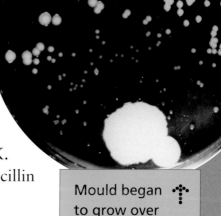

Mould began to grow over Fleming's dish.

Mould

Alexander Fleming made his discovery by mistake! It was all because he left the lid off of a bacteria-coated dish when he went on holiday. Thank goodness he did!

mould   type of fungus that grows in damp places
pneumonia   disease of the lungs that makes it difficult to breathe

Up to date

Each year we understand more about disease. We have made amazing progress in the last 30 years. But there is still plenty to learn.

AIDS

During the late 1970s, doctors in New York and California reported many cases of rare cancer and **pneumonia** in young men. These diseases were taking hold because the men's **immune systems** were failing. They seemed unable to fight infections. A new **virus** was making them ill.

In the early 1980s, the new condition caused by this HIV virus was named AIDS. This stands for Acquired Immune Deficiency Syndrome.

Did you know?

- More than 90 per cent of people with AIDS live in poor countries where sex education is often not available.
- Every minute, 5 people between the ages of 10 and 24 are infected with HIV somewhere in the world.

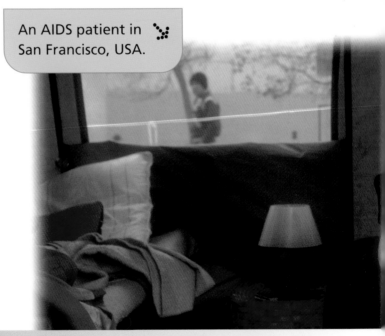

An AIDS patient in San Francisco, USA.

42

Word bank

orphan   someone, especially a child, whose parents are dead

HIV

Many people today carry the HIV virus. It does not always develop into AIDS. Unlike other viruses, HIV is not passed on by sneezing or touching. It can only infect through exchanging body fluids such as blood or **semen**.

If the virus develops into AIDS, the patient's immune system fails to fight infections properly. There is still no cure for the disease. More than 20 million people have died of AIDS. The number of people living with the HIV virus is now about 42 million.

AIDS orphans

- In the USA, AIDS makes about 125,000 children into **orphans** each year.
- In Africa, 23 million children have already lost their parents to AIDS.
- By 2010, over 40 million children will be orphaned by AIDS worldwide.
- The cost of treating someone with AIDS in the USA is well over US$100,000.

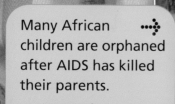

Many African children are orphaned after AIDS has killed their parents.

semen   fluid that contains sperm

One type of mosquito spreads a worm that does real damage to people. When it bites, the female mosquito injects tiny worm **larvae** into the bloodstream. The worm grows and causes a disease called **elephantiasis** that makes the legs swell up.

Parasites

Many tiny creatures live in or on the human body. Even clean human skin contains about 5 million **bacteria** per square centimetre.

At least 80 different kinds of bacteria live in the human mouth without causing harm. But larger **parasites** are killers in some parts of the world.

Some types of **worm** get inside humans in uncooked food. Tapeworms can grow up to 10 metres long inside people! Round worms are caught from infected water or food. These worms infect a **billion** people worldwide. They kill 20,000 people a year by blocking up their **intestines**.

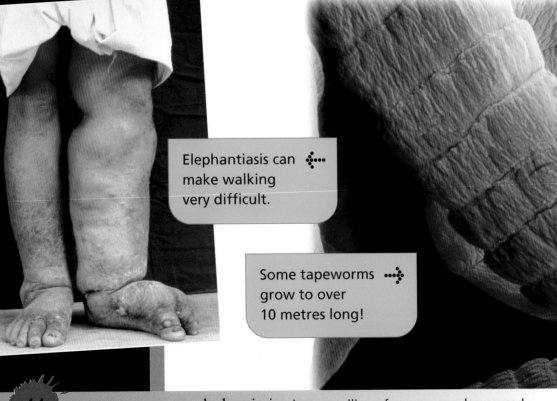

Elephantiasis can make walking very difficult.

Some tapeworms grow to over 10 metres long!

Word bank

elephantiasis   huge swelling of an arm or a leg caused by a type of worm

Malaria

Mosquitoes can be deadly. If an infected mosquito bites someone, it passes a **virus** into the blood. **Malaria** is a flu-like illness lasting between ten and twenty days. If it affects the kidneys or brain, it can kill.

In the last 2000 years, malaria may have caused half of all human deaths on the planet. Today many people survive malaria with modern drugs. Even so, it kills over a million people each year. In fact, more people today die from malaria than they did 30 years ago.

The deadly *Anopheles* mosquito spreads malaria.

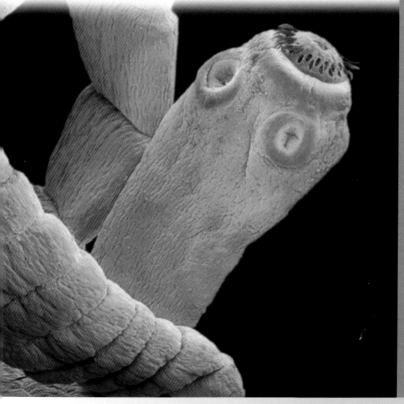

Did you know?

- Malaria now infects 300 million people each year. The young and old are at most risk of dying.
- Two children die of malaria every minute.
- Ninety per cent of all malaria cases are in Africa where it is the main cause of death in the 21st century.

parasite   living thing that lives or feeds on other living things, often harming them

Cancer news

One of the most feared diseases of modern times is cancer. It is feared because more people seem to develop it now. That is because we survive other diseases and live longer.

Cancer develops when **cells** begin to grow out of control inside the body. Although there are many kinds of cancer, they all start because of **abnormal** cells.

Cancer cells often form a **tumour**. Tumours can grow in most parts of the body. Some cancers, like **leukaemia**, affect the blood. Cancer cells often travel to other parts of the body, where they can grow and take over normal cells. This is how cancer spreads through the body.

Cancer researchers test anti-cancer drugs.

Word bank   abnormal   unusual and not normal

Progress

A third of people in richer countries get cancer at some time in their lives. One fifth of these die of the disease. Scientists are working hard to find out how cells develop cancer. By finding what triggers this, they hope to make new anti-cancer drugs.

Doctors are making great progress in treating the disease. When cancer is caught early, doctors today are often able to stop the cells from growing. The good news is that in the last 10 years, the death rate from cancer has fallen by 12 per cent.

Giant tumour

Marie Bell was seventeen in 1999 when she had stomach pains. She went to hospital in Maryland, USA where doctors found a 36-kilogram tumour in her ovary. It was the size of a beach ball. Four doctors removed the tumour in a four-hour operation.

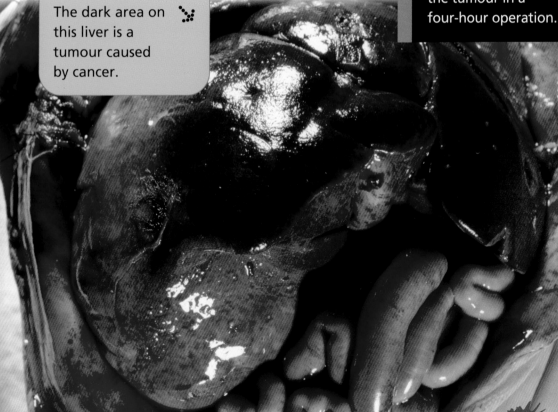

The dark area on this liver is a tumour caused by cancer.

leukaemia   type of cancer that affects the blood cells

Bird flu

Many diseases are no longer the problem they once were. The bad news is, some of the old diseases can **adapt**. New types of flu can suddenly break out. With modern air travel, a new **virus** can cross the world in a few hours.

We can still catch a few diseases from animals. Birds catch a type of flu and pass it on to humans. In 2004, people were worried about a new flu **epidemic** spread by birds. Bird flu started in Vietnam. The virus spread through hens in Asia. Eleven people died after catching the disease.

Super bugs

Antibiotics have saved many lives - but there is a problem. Each time a patient takes an antibiotic for an infection, the drug may not kill all the **bacteria**. A few may survive and adapt in order to beat the drug. These can breed to make super bugs that antibiotics cannot kill.

Nearly 5 million ⋯⋗ chickens had to be killed and buried in the bird flu outbreak in Vietnam in 2004.

48

Word bank

adapt   alter to fit in with new conditions, becoming slightly different

SARS

A new disease broke out in China in 2002. It was called SARS, which stands for Severe Acute **Respiratory** Syndrome. People worried that it might become a serious epidemic. In fact, only 8098 people caught SARS worldwide. Of these, 774 died.

People in Japan, China and Hong Kong wore medical masks in the streets. They were scared they would breathe in the new virus. In Ontario, Canada there was a big SARS scare. People were not allowed to travel for a while. This was to stop the disease from spreading.

People wear masks in a street in Hong Kong to protect them from SARS.

Mad cow disease

A new brain disease affected cows in the 1990s. Some people then developed a similar disease. They had probably eaten infected beef. This human form of the disease is called new variant CJD. Between 1996 and 2002, 129 people developed new variant CJD in the UK. There is no cure yet, and infected people will die.

respiratory   to do with breathing and the lungs

Latest developments

All around the world scientists are looking into different diseases. They are trying to find answers to health problems that have troubled humans for years.

There are signs of progress in fighting a **virus** that affects people in parts of Africa. A disease called **ebola**, which causes bleeding inside the body, kills over 75 per cent of its victims. At the moment there is no cure for this disease. But in 2004, scientists working on mice reported big steps that could lead to a safe human **vaccine** in the future.

Old and healthy

We are all living longer today than ever before. One disease that still affects old people today is called Alzheimer's. This is when the brain no longer works properly. But already scientists are developing new drugs that may help to keep Alzheimer's under control.

Many older people today keep healthy and active.

Word bank   digest   break food down into little bits

Breakthrough

A team of British scientists has been working on a vaccine for some types of cancer. An important step in 2004 was developing a vaccine against **leukaemia,** a cancer of the blood. Doctors tested the vaccine on mice with the disease and found the mice lived much longer as a result. It would be like humans having another 25 years of life.

The world awaits the next great discovery in the long war against disease. It is a fight that began thousands of years ago. The war is far from over, but many of the battles have already been won.

Healthy bacteria

Ninety-nine per cent of all **bacteria** are useful. Bacteria help our bodies **digest** food and make important **vitamins**. There are more bacteria in your body than there are people on the planet!

Scientists keep making new discoveries to fight disease.

ebola   disease causing rapid death through massive blood loss

Find out more

Did you know?

- Leprosy is the oldest known disease in the world. Cases of this nasty disease were first described in ancient Egypt as early as 1350 BC.

- There are 180 different types of the **virus** that causes the world's most infectious disease: the common cold.

Books

Groundbreakers: Alexander Fleming, Steve Parker (Heinemann Library, 2001)

Microlife: Fighting Infectious Diseases, Robert Sneddon (Heinemann Library, 2000)

Microlife: The Benefits of Bacteria, Robert Sneddon (Heinemann Library, 2000)

Using the Internet

Explore the Internet to find out more about medicine through the ages. You can use a search engine, such as www.yahooligans.com, and type in keywords such as:

- The Plague
- tuberculosis
- medicine + The American Civil War
- Louis Pasteur

Search tips

There are billions of pages on the Internet so it can be difficult to find exactly what you are looking for.

These search tips will help you find useful websites more quickly:

- Know exactly what you want to find out about first.
- Use two to six keywords in a search, putting the most important words first.
- Be precise. Only use names of people, places or things.

Glossary

abnormal unusual and not normal

adapt alter to fit in with new conditions, becoming slightly different

antibiotic substance made from bacteria that kills other harmful bacteria

antiseptic substance that stops harmful bacteria growing and spreading disease

bacteria group of tiny living things, some can cause disease

bile fluid made by the liver to help digestion

billion one thousand million

boil swollen infection on the skin that is red and sore

bowel part of the intestine where waste is held before being let out of the body

buboes swollen areas in the groin and armpits

cells tiny building blocks that make up all living things

cesspit hole dug to hold waste and sewage

cholera disease causing severe stomach upset, which can kill

coma like being in a deep sleep, usually caused by injury or disease

consumption another name for the disease tuberculosis

diarrhoea the need to use the toilet very often (when waste is too liquid)

digest break food down into little bits

diptheria disease causing a high fever and making your throat so swollen that breathing is difficult

dung waste matter (manure) from an animal

ebola disease causing rapid death through massive blood loss

electron microscope microscope using electron beams to make images much larger

elephantiasis huge swelling of an arm or a leg caused by a type of worm

epidemic outbreak of a disease that spreads quickly over a wide area

excrement body waste

fever very high body temperature caused by illness

glands parts of the body that make different chemicals

hygiene standards of cleanliness

immune system the body's way of defending itself against disease

immunity the body's protection against disease

infectious spreads easily from one person to another

intestine part of the body that goes from the stomach to the bowel, where food is digested

larvae immature form of an insect or worm

leukaemia type of cancer that affects the blood cells

malaria disease that causes fever and chills, spread by mosquito bites

mass graves huge graves where lots of people were buried together

Middle Ages period of history roughly between AD 500 and AD 1500

monk member of a religious community of men

mosquito tiny fly that sucks blood from animals and people and can spread disease

mould type of fungus that grows in damp places

Native American member of any tribe of North American Indian in the USA

nervous system how messages are sent around the body from the brain

Nobel Prize international prize awarded for outstanding work

organism living cell or group of cells

orphan someone, especially a child, whose parents are dead

pandemic disease that spreads quickly across the world

paralysis unable to move

parasite living thing that lives or feeds on other living things, often harming them

phlegm thick fluid in the lungs and throat

plague deadly disease that spreads quickly

pneumonia disease of the lungs that makes it difficult to breathe

pockmark round scar left on the skin after a pox disease

pollute make air or water dirty or unsafe

pox any disease that causes a rash of pus-filled spots

pus thick yellow or greenish foul-smelling liquid made by infected wounds

red blood cells tiny cells in the blood that carry oxygen round the body

respiratory to do with breathing and the lungs

saliva spit and fluid inside the mouth

scrofula disease causing swellings, common in the Middle Ages

scurvy killer disease causing swollen, bleeding gums – due to a lack of vitamin C

semen fluid that contains sperm

senna powder made from the seeds of the cassia tree

sewage waste and dirty water from toilets

slums poor, dirty housing in overcrowded parts of a city

smallpox infectious disease causing blisters all over the body

spasm sudden, uncontrolled movement of muscles

spinal cord bundle of nerves that run down the backbone

suffocation unable to breathe

superstition belief based on magic or chance

tribe group of people living closely together, sharing the same beliefs and customs

tuberculosis disease that causes fever and lung failure

tumour abnormal growth or swelling in the body

typhoid disease spread by eating food or water with bacteria in it

ulcer open sore, often full of pus

urine liquid passed from the body, usually pale yellow

vaccine medicine to make the body defend itself against a disease

virus tiny living thing that breaks into the body's cells and can cause disease

vitamin substance needed in small amounts in our food to keep us healthy

volunteer someone who offers to take part in something

well hole dug down into the ground for getting water

whooping cough disease causing coughing fits and breathing difficulties

worm kind of parasite that lives in the human body

yellow fever disease spread by mosquitoes, causing fever, aching limbs and yellow skin

Index

Titles in the *Painful History of Medicine* series include:

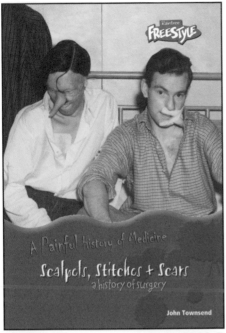

Hardback   1-844-43750-7

Hardback   1-844-43751-5

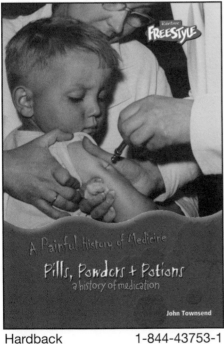

Hardback   1-844-43753-1

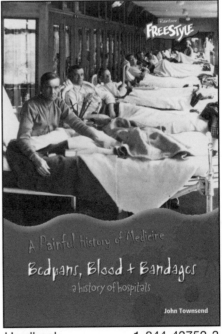

Hardback   1-844-43752-3

Find out about the other titles in this series on our website www.raintreepublishers.co.uk